WARM THE WALLS WITH QUILTS

Oxmoor House®

WARM THE WALLS WITH QUILTS

©1996 by Oxmoor House, Inc.

Book Division of Southern Progress Corporation
P.O. Box 2463, Birmingham, AL 35201

Published by Oxmoor House, Inc., and
Leisure Arts, Inc.

Library of Congress Catalog Number: 95-72157
ISBN: 0-8487-1278-1

Manufactured in the United States of America
First Printing 1996

Editor-in-Chief: Nancy Fitzpatrick Wyatt
Editorial Director, Special Interest Publications:
   Ann H. Harvey
Senior Crafts Editor: Susan Ramey Cleveland
Senior Editor, Editorial Services: Olivia Kindig Wells
Art Director: James Boone

WARM THE WALLS WITH QUILTS

Editor: Rhonda Richards Wamble
Editorial Assistant: Wendy Wolford Noah
Copy Editor: Jennifer K. Mathews
Senior Designer: Larry Hunter
Designer: Carol Loria
Illustrator: Kelly Davis
Publishing Systems Administrator: Rick Tucker
Senior Photographer: John O'Hagan
Photo Stylist: Katie Stoddard
Production and Distribution Director: Phillip Lee
Associate Production Managers: Theresa L. Beste,
   Vanessa D. Cobbs
Production Coordinator: Marianne Jordan Wilson
Production Assistant: Valerie Heard

Contents

Dear Quilting Friends,

A century ago, women hung their quilts over walls and windows to keep out icy winter winds and drafts. While our modern climate-controlled homes make this practice unnecessary, we still like to display our handiwork on our walls. Quilters in the last quarter of the twentieth century have brought status to quilts as an art form. These days you're likely to see quilts hanging in public buildings and businesses as well as in homes.

You'll find the 11 lovely quilt designs on the following pages perfect for gracing your walls or those of your friends and family. Why not try Georgia Bonesteel's *Hillside Village* on page 15 or Flavin Glover's *Hemlocks* on page 18? If you're in a holiday mood, you might like to deck your walls with Judy Sogn's *Christmas Tulips* on page 42. Looking for a great design to stitch a wallhanging for your husband's office? Check out Lara Kline's *Cranberry Flying Geese* on page 12.

After you've made your masterpiece, read Hanging Your Quilt on page 23 for tips on how to hang your quilt. We tell you not only how to show the quilt to its best advantage but also the best hanging techniques to avoid damage.

Happy stitching,

Susan Ramey Cleveland

WORKSHOP

Selecting Fabrics

The best fabric for quilts is 100% cotton. Yardage requirements are based on 44"-wide fabric and allow for shrinkage. All fabrics, including backing, should be machine-washed, dried, and pressed before cutting. Use warm water and detergent but not fabric softener.

Necessary Notions

- Scissors
- Rotary cutter and mat
- Acrylic rulers
- Template plastic
- Pencils for marking cutting lines
- Sewing needles
- Sewing thread
- Sewing machine
- Seam ripper
- Pins
- Iron and ironing board
- Quilting needles
- Thimble
- Hand quilting thread
- Machine quilting thread

Making Templates

A template is a duplication of a printed pattern, made from a sturdy material, which is traced onto fabric. Many regular shapes such as squares and triangles can be marked directly on the fabric with a ruler, but you need templates for other shapes. Some quiltmakers use templates for all shapes.

You can trace patterns directly onto template plastic. Or make a template by tracing a pattern onto graph paper and gluing the paper to posterboard or sandpaper. (Sandpaper will not slip on fabric.)

When a large pattern is given in two pieces, make one template for the complete piece.

Cut out the template on the marked line. It is important that a template be traced, marked, and cut accurately. If desired, punch out corner dots with a ⅛"-diameter hole punch (**Diagram 1**).

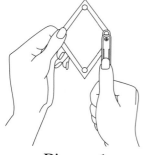

Diagram 1

Mark each template with its letter and grain line. Verify the template's accuracy, placing it over the printed pattern. Any discrepancy, however small, is multiplied many times as the quilt is assembled. Another way to check templates' accuracy is to make a test block before cutting more pieces.

Tracing Templates on Fabric

For hand piecing, templates should be cut to the finished size of the piece so seam lines can be marked on the fabric. Avoiding the selvage, place the template *facedown* on the *wrong* side of the fabric, aligning the template grain line with the straight grain. Hold the template firmly and trace around it. Repeat as needed, leaving ½" between tracings (**Diagram 2**).

Diagram 2

For machine piecing, templates should include seam allowances. These templates are used in the same manner as for hand piecing, but you can mark the fabric using common lines for efficient cutting (**Diagram 3**). Mark corners on fabric through holes in the template.

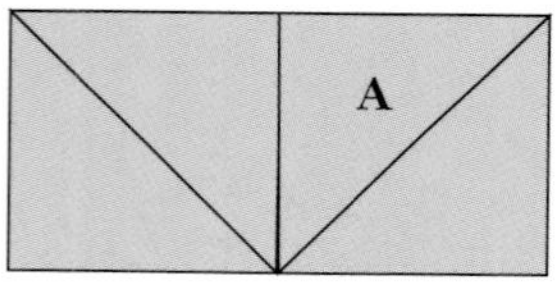

Diagram 3

For hand or machine piecing, use window templates to enhance accuracy by drawing and cutting out both cutting and sewing lines. The guidance of a drawn seam line is very useful for sewing set-in seams, when pivoting at a precise point is critical. Used on the right side of the fabric, window templates help you cut specific motifs with accuracy (**Diagram 4**).

Diagram 4

For hand appliqué, templates should be made the finished size. Place templates *faceup* on the *right* side of the fabric. Position tracings at least ½" apart (**Diagram 5**). Add a ¼" seam allowance around pieces when cutting.

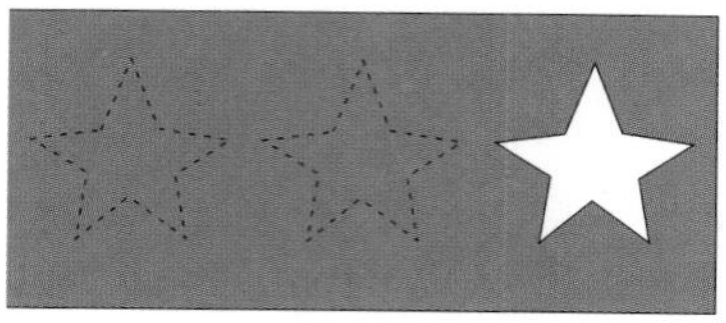

Diagram 5

Finished Quilt Size

56" x 62"

Number of Blocks and Finished Size

255 Rail Fence blocks   3" x 3"

Fabric Requirements

Assorted dark greens	1½ yards
Assorted browns	½ yard
Assorted light greens	1¼ yards
Assorted creams	2 yards
Dark green	1¾ yards
Brown	2½ yards*
Backing	3¾ yards

*Includes fabric for straight-grain binding.

Number to Cut

Rail (cut 1½" x 3½" pieces)
393 dark greens
79 assorted browns
190 light greens
432 creams

Number to Make

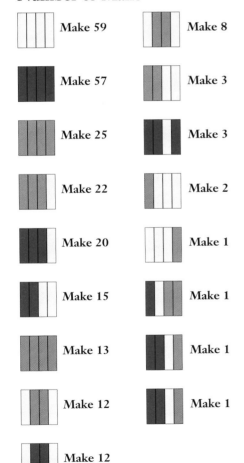

Make 59
Make 57
Make 25
Make 22
Make 20
Make 15
Make 13
Make 12
Make 12

Make 8
Make 3
Make 3
Make 2
Make 1
Make 1
Make 1
Make 1

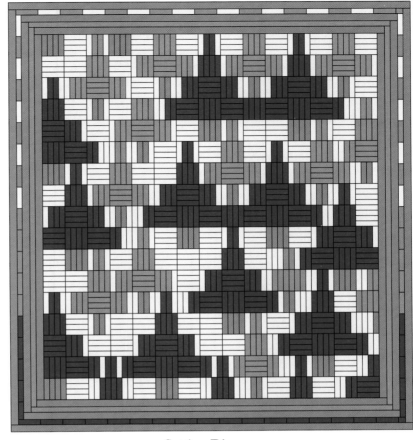

Setting Diagram

Quilt Top Assembly

1. Join 4 rails to make 1 Rail Fence block. Make 265 blocks according to Number to Make. You will have 74 rails left over for border.

2. Join Rail Fence blocks into 17 rows of 15, referring to **Setting Diagram** for placement. Join rows.

3. From brown, cut 2 (1½" x 51½") border strips. Join to opposite sides of quilt. Cut 2 (1½" x 47½") lengthwise border strips. Join to top and bottom edges of quilt, butting corners.

4. From dark green, cut 2 (1½" x 53½") lengthwise border strips. Join to opposite sides of quilt. Cut 2 (1¼" x 49") lengthwise border strips. Join to top and bottom edges of quilt, butting corners.

5. From brown, cut 2 (1½" x 55") lengthwise border strips. Join to opposite sides of quilt. Cut 2 (1½" x 51") lengthwise border strips. Join to top and bottom edges of quilt, butting corners.

6. To make fourth border, join assorted green and cream rails end to end. You will use 74 rails: 19 along the top and bottom and 18 along the sides. Trim excess. Flavin arranged the rails so that they went from the darkest greens at the bottom to lighter greens and creams on the sides and top.

7. From brown, cut 2 (2½" x 58") lengthwise border strips. Join to sides of quilt. Cut 2 (1½" x 56½") lengthwise border strips. Join to top and bottom edges of quilt, butting corners.

Quilting

Outline-quilt inside seam lines of tree trunks, background, and borders, or quilt as desired.

Finished Edges

Referring to instructions on page 11, make 7 yards of 2"-wide straight-grain binding from brown. Apply binding to quilt edges.

Quilt by Mary Ruth Branyon
Landrum, South Carolina

Starlit Flower Garden

Mary Ruth Branyon's garden quilt grew out of a special floral fabric. The print became the center of the nine-patch block, Fifty-four Forty or Fight. Alternating that block with a variation of Star Daze in a block-to-block setting created a blue Orange Peel design. The four-patch squares and the diagonally pieced squares are perfect places to use quick-piecing techniques. Use a 4½" square as a master template to check each patch.

Finished Quilt Size

76" x 76"

Number of Blocks and Finished Size

13 Fifty-four Forty
or Fight blocks   12" x 12"
12 Star Daze blocks   12" x 12"

Fabric Requirements

Floral print	⅝ yard
Cream	2 yards
Rose	2¼ yards
Blue	3½ yards*
Pink	½ yard
Backing	5 yards

*Includes fabric for straight-grain binding.

Number to Cut**

Template A	29 floral print
[Or rotary-cut 29 (4½") squares.]	
Template B	108 cream
Template C	56 rose 52 blue
Template C rev.	56 rose 52 blue
Template D	48 cream 48 blue

[Or rotary-cut 24 (4⅞") squares
of each. Cut each square in half
diagonally to make 48 triangles
of each color.]

Template E	112 rose 112 pink

[Or rotary-cut 112 (2½")
squares of each.]

**See steps 1 and 2 to cut borders before
cutting other pieces.

Quilt Top Assembly

1. From rose, cut 8 (4½" x
16½") and 4 (4½" x 20½") strips
for inner border. Set aside.

2. From blue, cut 4 (4½" x
68½") border strips. Set aside.

3. Referring to **Star Daze
Diagram,** join pieces as shown to
make 12 blocks. You should have 8
cream Bs and 16 rose Cs remaining. Join these into 8 B/C units.
Set aside for use in borders.

4. Referring to **Fifty-four Forty
or Fight Diagram,** join pieces as
shown to make 13 blocks. (*Note:*
Refer to **Setting Diagram** for
direction of four-patch units.) You
should have 8 rose Es and 8 pink

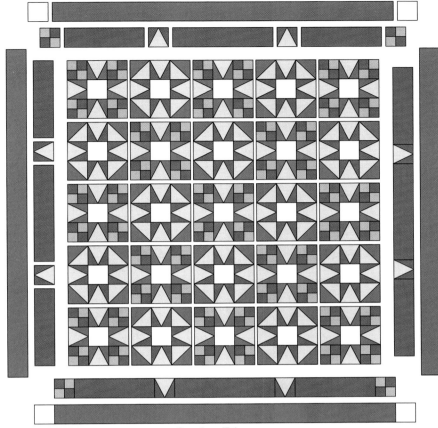

Setting Diagram

Es remaining. Join into four-patch
units. Set aside for use in borders.

5. Referring to **Setting Diagram,**
alternate blocks as shown to make
horizontal rows. Join rows.

6. Referring to **Setting
Diagram,** join 1 (4½" x 16½")
rose strip, 1 B/C unit from Step 3,
1 (4½" x 20½") rose strip, 1 B/C
unit, and 1 (4½" x 16½") rose strip
into 1 long row for inner side border. Repeat to make 4 borders. Join
1 border to each side of quilt.

Referring to **Setting Diagram,**
join four-patch units made in Step
4 to opposite ends of remaining 2

borders. Join borders to top and
bottom edges of quilt.

7. Join 2 (4½" x 68½") blue borders to opposite sides of quilt. Join
2 As to opposite ends of remaining
2 borders. Join borders to top and
bottom edges of quilt.

Quilting

Quilt as desired.

Finished Edges

Referring to instructions on page
11, make 9 yards of 2"-wide
straight-grain binding from blue.
Apply binding to quilt edges.

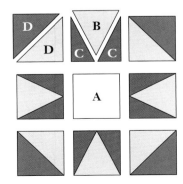

Star Daze Diagram

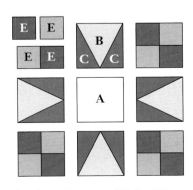

Fifty-four Forty or Fight Diagram

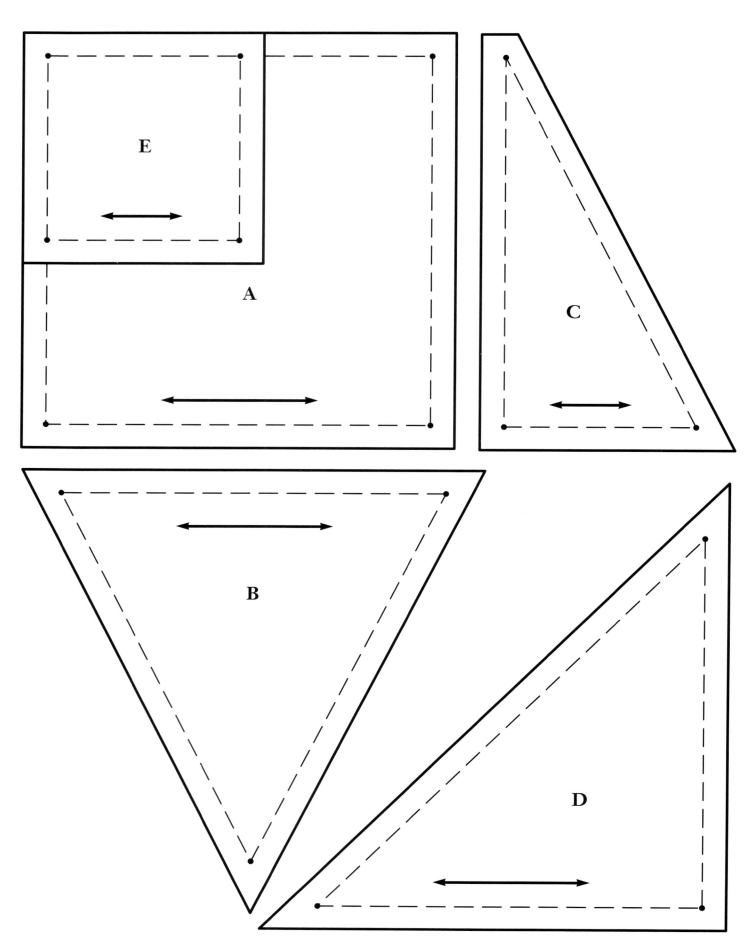

E

A

C

B

D

Hanging Your Quilt

Make sure you consider your quilt's safety when choosing a hanging method.

Displaying Your Quilts

If you are like most quilters, there will come a time when you will run out of beds on which to place your handiwork. Hanging a quilt on a wall is another attractive way to display it. Choose a hanging technique that will not damage your treasure. Look for wall racks with clamps that hold quilts safely, or simply use a rod and a hanging sleeve (see below).

To hang a quilt, run a wooden dowel, a PVC pipe, or a curtain rod through the sleeve and hang it from brackets on the wall. Be sure to coat unfinished wooden dowels with polyurethane varnish to protect the fabric from acids in the wood.

Never hang your quilt for more than three months at a time. Because hanging strains the seams of a quilt, rest the quilt regularly. Place a piece of furniture or other barrier in front of the displayed quilt to discourage touching. Skin contains oils and minerals that can accumulate on a quilt and deteriorate the fabric.

Quilts can brighten any room where there is a little extra wall space. Whenever possible, try to hang your quilts on an inside wall away from direct sunlight. The harmful rays of the sun can fade your quilt, even after only a year or so. If the quilt has only partial sun exposure, it can fade unevenly. If your quilt must hang in an area that receives sunlight, try to close the curtains or blinds during the sun's peak hours. Or, if you are decorating with seasonal quilts, rotate different quilts in that location to even the wear.

Making a Hanging Sleeve

Quilts that are hung for wall display should have a sleeve attached to the back. A dowel or curtain rod, slipped through the sleeve, can hang from brackets on the wall.

1. Cut a 6"-wide fabric piece that measures the width of the quilt plus 2". Turn under a ¼" hem on each end and press; then turn under 1" more. Press and topstitch.

2. With wrong sides facing, join long edges. Press the seam allowances open, centering the seam on one side of the tube. With the seam facing the quilt backing, place the sleeve just below the binding at the top of the quilt, centering it between the quilt sides (**Diagram**).

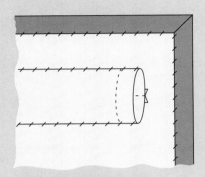

Diagram

3. Slipstitch the top and bottom edges of the sleeve to the quilt backing only, making sure no stitches go through to the quilt top.

Winona Winter II

Ann Fahl used real leaves that she picked from trees at her cottage on Winona Lake, Indiana, for the leaf patterns in *Winona Winter II.* "The simple theme of triangles, tulle, and snowy white leaves was meant to get my creativity recharged at the end of a long winter," Ann says.

Quilt by Ann Fahl
Racine, Wisconsin

24

Finished Quilt Size

60" x 37½"

Fabric Requirements

Assorted dark red prints	1¼ yards
Assorted medium red prints	2½ yards
Assorted blue prints	1¼ yards
Assorted purple prints	⅔ yard
Lavender print	¾ yard*
White	½ yard
Blue/white stripe	½ yard
Navy	¼ yard
White tulle (optional)	¼ yard
Backing	2½ yards

*Includes ½ yard for binding.

Number to Cut

Template A	72	dark red prints
	148	medium red prints
	62	blue prints
	38	purple prints
Template B	6	lavender print
Template C	7	white
	1	blue/white stripe
Template D	2	white
	7	blue/white stripe
Template E	9	blue/white stripe
	11	navy
Template F	23	white
	4	blue/white stripe

Ann embellished Winona Winter II *with layered tulle (also called "bridal illusion" and available in the bridal department of fabric stores) to recall wintry skies. She also heavily machine-quilted the background using contrasting thread; she added beads in places "to give the sparkle of ice to the quilt," she says.*

Quilt Top Assembly

1. Referring to **Setting Diagram** and photograph for color placement, join 32 As in pairs to make 16 squares as shown. Join squares to make 1 row. Repeat to make 10 rows, referring to photograph for color placement. Join rows.

2. If desired, cut edges of white tulle in random curves to suggest a snowy effect. Place tulle on quilt top; straightstitch edges to secure. (Because tulle does not ravel, edges need not be turned under or otherwise finished.)

3. Referring to photograph for guidance, arrange Bs, Cs, Ds, Es, and Fs in pleasing arrangement across quilt top. Pin pieces in place. Appliqué each piece to quilt top.

Quilting

Outline-quilt around each appliquéd leaf. Quilt remainder in-the-ditch, or quilt as desired.

Finished Edges

Referring to instructions on page 11, make 5¾ yards of 2"-wide bias or straight-grain binding from lavender print. Apply binding to quilt edges.

Setting Diagram

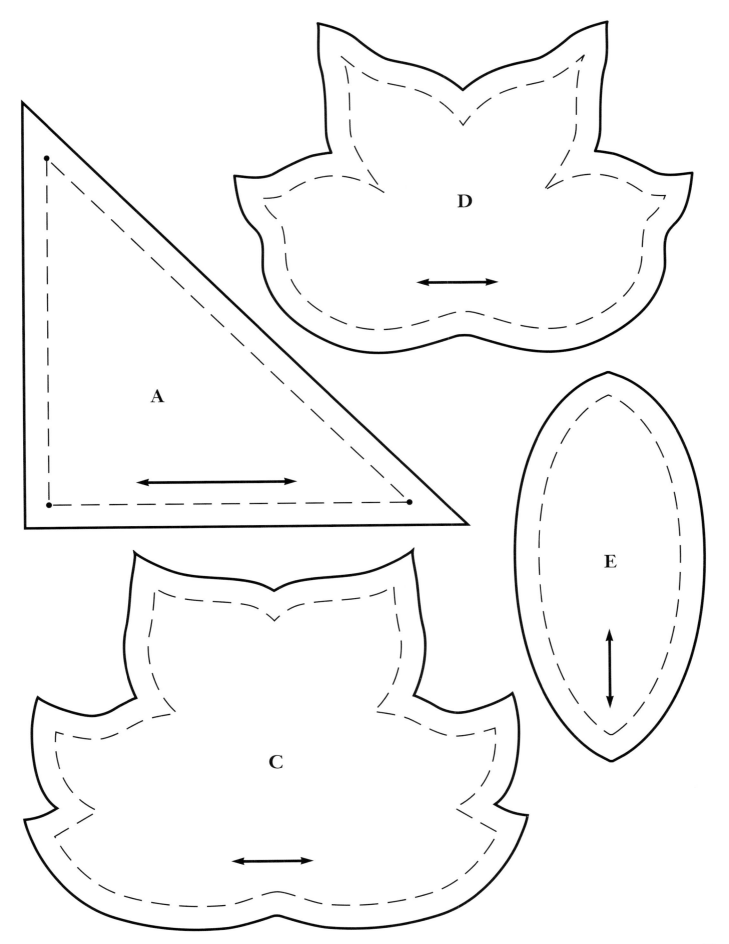

27

F

B

28

Finished Quilt Size

62½" x 80"

Fabric Requirements

Orange to blue
(18 values)   ½ yard each
Blue for bias binding   1 yard
Backing and facing   5½ yards

Other Materials

Bicycle clips
Thread to match backing (for
machine quilting)

Quilt Top Assembly

1. Cut each fabric into 3"-wide
crosswise strips. Cut strips into 3"
squares.

2. Arrange squares in 25 vertical
rows, as shown in **Setting
Diagram.** (Note that row arrangement has an 8-row repeat.)

Make 41 prairie points from
light blue and attach to top of
squares with ¼" seam, as shown in
Setting Diagram. Stack squares in
rows; label rows as shown.

3. Join squares to form rows.
Iron seam allowances of odd-
numbered rows up and even-
numbered rows down. Join rows.

Channel Quilting

Layer quilt as described on page
10. Do not baste. Fold quilt top
back from right to left to expose
vertical seam allowance of Row 1.
Smooth quilt top and place straight
pins at top of Row 1 seam
allowance and at seam allowance
intersections of each square. (Insert
pins through all layers.)

Roll batting and backing on right
so that quilt will fit under arm of
sewing machine. Secure roll with
bicycle clips.

Attach walking foot to sewing
machine and use thread to match
quilt backing. Sew directly on
stitching of row seam allowance.

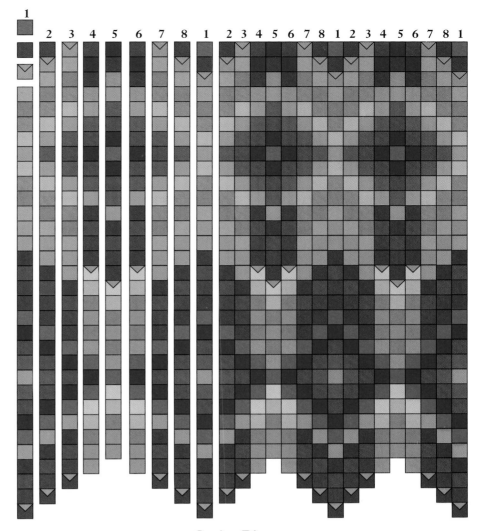

Setting Diagram

(Stitching attaches quilt top to quilt
layers so that it shows only on the
back.) Continue in same manner
for all rows.

Finished Edges

Because of the stair-step bottom
edge, Katy suggests stitching a facing to it for a clean-finished edge.
Cut facing for bottom of quilt,
13" x 63", from backing fabric.
Turn 1 long edge under ¼" to
wrong side and press.

With right sides facing, match

raw edge of bottom (lowest)
squares to raw edge of facing, as
shown in **Facing Diagram.** Join
facing to quilt, following stair-step
edge of quilt. Trim facing even
with quilt. Turn facing to quilt
back, clipping corners as needed,
and blindstitch folded edge to
backing.

Referring to instructions on page
11, make 6½ yards of bias binding
from blue. Apply binding to
remaining 3 sides of quilt.

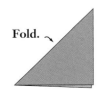

Fold.

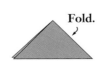

Fold.

Prairie Points Diagram

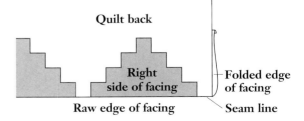

Quilt back

Right
side of facing

Raw edge of facing

Folded edge
of facing

Seam line

Facing Diagram

Quilt by Karen K. Buckley
Carlisle, Pennsylvania

Joe's Quilt

This quilt began when Karen K. Buckley's husband, Joe, commented that she had never made a quilt for him. "Of all the things you have quilted and given away," he said to Karen, "you never have made me a quilt." That was enough to start Karen sewing! Since she was in a hurry to complete a quilt for Joe, she developed a strip-piecing method to cut assembly time. Joe proudly displays his quilt on his office wall.

Finished Quilt Size
45½" x 45½"

Number of Blocks and Finished Size
9 blocks   10" x 10"

Fabric Requirements

Teal	⅜ yard
Teal print	¼ yard
Brown print	⅞ yard
Cream print	¾ yard
Brown paisley print	2 yards*
Backing	2¾ yards

*Includes 1 yard for binding.

Quilt Top Assembly

1. From teal and teal print, cut 1 (2¼"-wide) crosswise strip each. Join strips lengthwise to form a panel, as shown in **Block Piecing Diagram 1.** Cut 18 segments across panel seam line at 2¼" intervals. Position segments to form four-patch unit, as shown in **Block Piecing Diagram 1.** Repeat to make 9 four-patch units.

2. From brown print, cut 2 (2¼"-wide) crosswise strips. Cut 18 segments at 4" intervals. Join strips to opposite sides of four-patch units, as shown in **Block Piecing Diagram 2.**

3. From brown print, cut 1 (4"-wide) strip. From teal and teal print, cut 1 (2¼"-wide) crosswise strip each. Join strips lengthwise, as shown in **Block Piecing Diagram 3.** Cut 18 segments across panel seam lines at 2¼" intervals. Join segments to opposite sides of block, rotating strips as shown in **Block Piecing Diagram 4.**

4. From cream print, cut 3 (5⅞"-wide) crosswise strips. Cut strips into 18 (5⅞") squares. Cut squares in half diagonally to make 36 triangles. Join triangles to 2 opposite sides of each block. Press. Then join triangles to remaining sides, as shown in **Block Piecing Diagram 5.** Repeat to make 9 blocks.

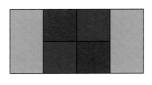

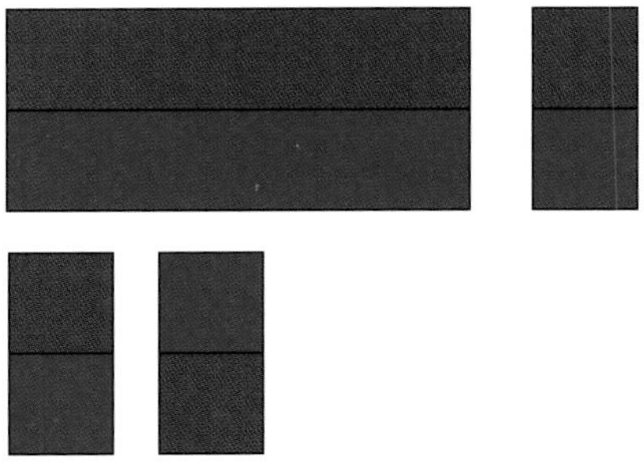

Block Piecing Diagram 1   **Block Piecing Diagram 2**

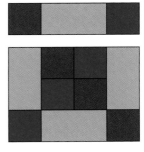

Block Piecing Diagram 3   **Block Piecing Diagram 4**

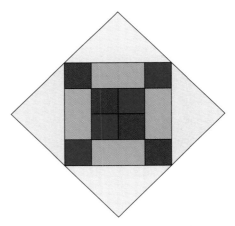

Block Piecing Diagram 5

5. From brown paisley print, cut 4 (2¼"-wide) crosswise strips. Cut strips into 72 (2¼") squares.

From brown print, cut 6 (2⅝"-wide) crosswise strips. Cut strips into 96 (2⅝") squares. Cut squares in half diagonally to make 192 triangles.

From teal, cut 2 (2⅝"-wide) crosswise strips. Cut strips into 32 (2⅝") squares. Cut squares in half diagonally to make 64 triangles.

Referring to **Sashing Diagram,** join 3 squares with 10 triangles to form sashing. Repeat to make 24

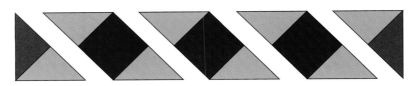

Sashing Diagram

Setting Diagram

sashing strips. You will have 16 teal triangles remaining. Set these aside.

6. Alternate 4 sashing strips with 3 blocks to form block row, as shown in **Setting Diagram.** Make 3 rows.

From cream print, cut 2 (3"-wide) crosswise strips. Cut strips into 16 (3") squares.

Alternate 4 cream print squares with 3 sashing strips to form a sashing row, as shown in **Setting Diagram.** Make 4 rows. Join sashing rows to block rows as shown.

7. From brown paisley print, cut 4 (1¾"-wide) crosswise strips. Cut 12 segments at 13¾" intervals. Trim ends of each segment at a 45° angle, as shown in **Border Strip Diagram.**

Alternate 4 teal triangles with 3 strips, as shown in **Setting Diagram,** and join to make a pieced border. Make 4 and set aside.

8. From brown paisley print, cut 4 (2" x 39¼") strips. Trim ends at 45° angle, as in Step 7. Join border strips to pieced border, as shown in **Setting Diagram.** Join borders to quilt.

9. From brown paisley print, cut 1 (6⅜"-wide) strip. Cut strip into 2 (6⅜") squares. Cut squares in half diagonally to make 4 triangles. Join

triangles to corners of quilt, as shown in **Setting Diagram.**

Quilting

Outline-quilt ¼" inside seam line of all triangles and squares. Quilt a 1" cross-hatching pattern in cream print triangles.

Finished Edges

Referring to instructions on page 11, make 5½ yards of 2"-wide straight-grain or bias binding from brown paisley print. Apply binding to quilt edges.

Trim.

Border Strip Diagram

36

Quilt by Merrilyn O. San Soucie
Newmarket, New Hampshire

Cyclical Basketry

Merrilyn O. San Soucie used fabric and color to express the cyclical changing of the seasons in her quilt *Cyclical Basketry*. The borders are Merrilyn's original patchwork design. She planned them to incorporate the four main color groups in the quilt and enhance the central design. Choose fabrics for this quilt that are nearly equal in print size and value. Review the Number to Cut for Baskets section (page 38) and the quilt photograph before selecting fabrics.

Finished Quilt Size
34⅝" x 34⅝"

Number of Blocks and Finished Size
4 Basket blocks   8" x 8"

Fabric Requirements

Muslin	⅝ yard
Green print 1	⅜ yard
Green print 2	⅛ yard
Dark green print	⅛ yard
Yellow print	⅜ yard
Peach print	⅛ yard
Brown print	¼ yard
Tan print	⅜ yard
Beige/brown print 1	¼ yard
Beige/brown print 2	⅛ yard
Beige/gray print	⅛ yard
Gray print 1	⅜ yard
Gray print 2	⅛ yard
Dark rust print	⅛ yard
Umber	⅛ yard
Muslin	1 yard*
Backing	1¼ yards

*Includes fabric for binding.

Number to Cut for Baskets

Yellow Basket

Template A	1 yellow print
Template B	1 muslin
Template C	1 yellow print
Template D	1 yellow print
	1 beige/brown print 1
Template D rev.	1 yellow print
	1 beige/brown print 1
Template E	1 yellow print
Template G	2 peach print
Template H	2 muslin
Template I	1 yellow print
	1 muslin
Template J	4 yellow print

Green Basket

Template A	1 dark green print
Template B	1 muslin
Template C	1 green print 1
Template D	1 green print 1
	1 green print 2
Template D rev.	1 green print 1
	1 green print 2
Template E	1 green print 1
Template G	2 dark green print
Template H	2 muslin
Template I	1 green print 1
	1 muslin
Template J	4 green print 1

Brown Basket

Template A	1 brown print
Template B	1 muslin
Template C	1 tan print
Template D	1 tan print
	1 beige/brown print 2
Template D rev.	1 tan print
	1 beige/brown print 2
Template E	1 tan print
Template G	2 brown print
Template H	2 muslin
Template I	1 tan print
	1 muslin
Template J	4 tan print

Gray Basket

Template A	1 beige/gray print
Template B	1 muslin
Template C	1 gray print 1
Template D	1 gray print 1
	1 beige/gray print
Template D rev.	1 gray print 1
	1 beige/gray print
Template E	1 gray print 1
Template G	2 gray print 2
Template H	2 muslin
Template I	1 gray print 1
	1 muslin
Template J	4 gray print 1

Number to Cut for Remainder of Quilt

Template C	8 green print 1
	8 dark rust print
Template D	4 dark rust print
Template D rev.	4 dark rust print
Template E	4 muslin
	8 beige/brown print 1
	8 gray print 1
Template F	4 muslin
Template I	4 brown print
Template K	8 tan print
	8 yellow print
	16 gray print 1
	16 muslin
Template L	16 beige/brown print 1
Template M	8 green print 1
	4 tan print
	4 yellow print
Template M rev.	8 beige/brown print 1
	4 tan print
	4 yellow print
Template N	16 muslin
Template O	8 brown print
Template P	8 yellow print
	4 green print 1
Template Q	4 peach print
Template Q rev.	4 peach print
Template R	4 umber
Template S	8 muslin
Template T	4 muslin
8½" square	1 muslin

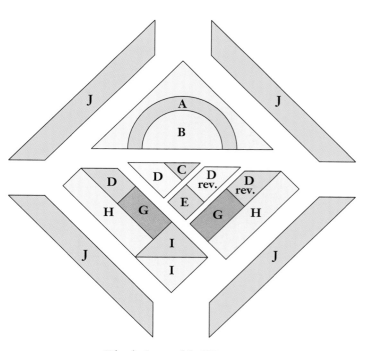

Block Assembly Diagram

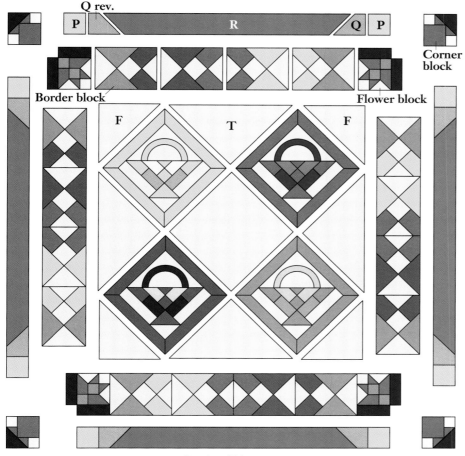

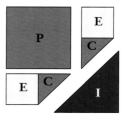

Corner block

Border block

Flower block

Q rev.

Setting Diagram

flower blocks to ends of remaining borders. Join borders to top and bottom edges of quilt as shown.

6. Join pieces as shown in **Corner Block Assembly Dia-**

Corner Block Assembly Diagram

gram. Make 4 corner blocks.

Join P, Q, and R for border strips, as shown in **Setting Diagram.** (*Note:* Add 16" between template R pieces to make full template.) Join borders to quilt sides; then join borders to top and bottom edges of quilt.

Set in corner blocks by stitching from the outside edge up to the seam line. Stop and backstitch 1 or 2 stitches. Remove fabric from machine. Align remaining sides and stitch from center to outside edge, backstitching 1 or 2 stitches at the start.

Quilting

Outline-quilt outside seam lines of all basket pieces. Outline-quilt ¼" inside seam lines of all border pieces. Quilt basket design in muslin center square. Quilt half-baskets in Ts. Quilt flower motif from flower block in each F.

Finished Edges

Referring to instructions on page 11, make 4 yards of bias or straight-grain binding from muslin. Apply binding to quilt edges.

Quilt Top Assembly

1. Sort pieces into groups for basket blocks as listed in Number to Cut for Baskets. Join pieces as shown in **Block Assembly Diagram.**

2. Join Fs and Ts to basket blocks, as shown in **Setting Diagram.**

3. Join K, L, M, and N to make pieced border rectangles, as shown in **Border Assembly Diagram.** Make 4 using gray print 1 Ks with tan print Ms; make 4 using tan

print Ks with green print 1 Ms; make 4 using yellow print Ks with green print 1 Ms; make 4 using gray print 1 Ks with yellow print Ms.

4. Join pieces, as shown in **Flower Block Assembly Diagram.** Make 4 flower blocks, 2 regular and 2 reversed.

5. Arrange border rectangles and flower blocks, as shown in quilt photograph and **Setting Diagram.**

Join 4 border rectangles, as shown, for each border. Join 2 borders to opposite sides of quilt. Join

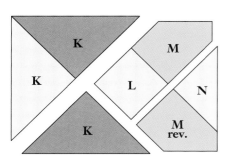

Border Assembly Diagram

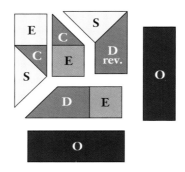

Flower Block Assembly Diagram

39

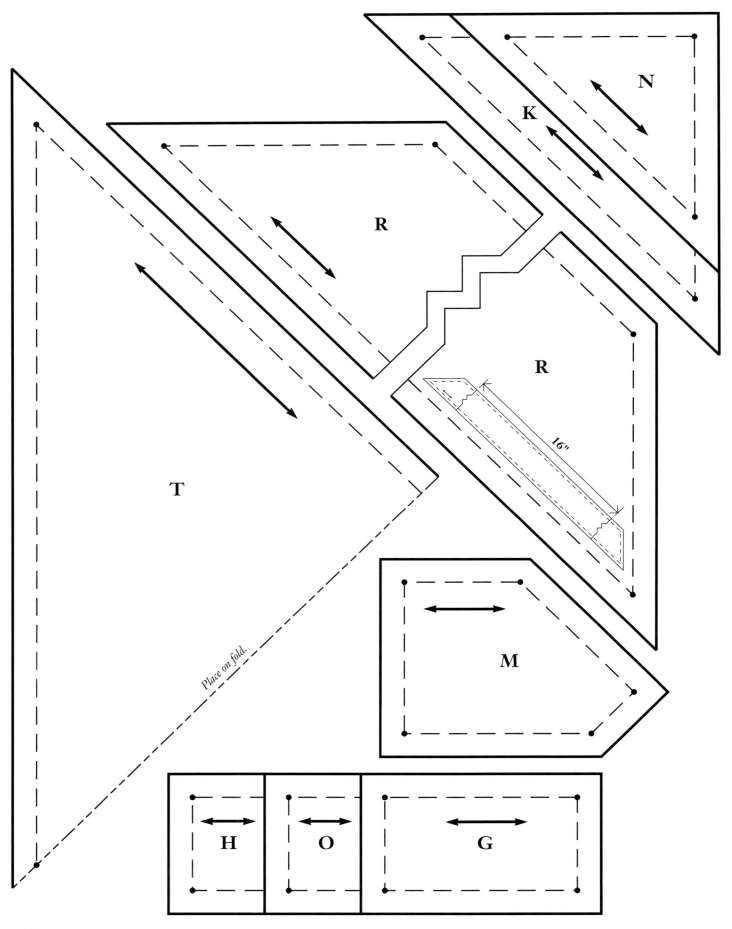

N

K

R

R

16"

T

Place on fold.

M

H   O   G

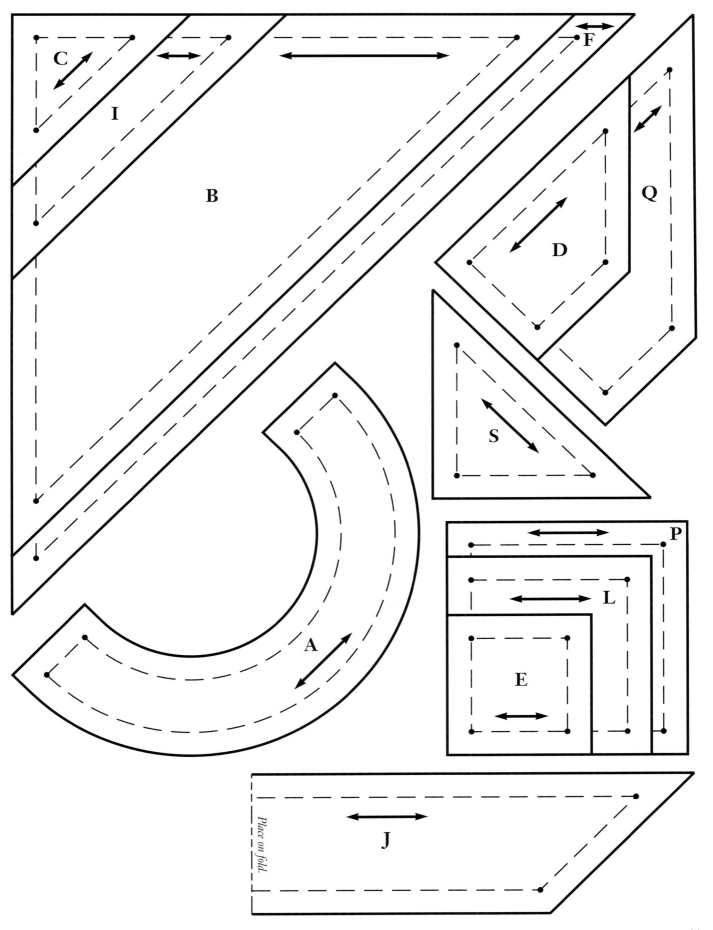

C

I

B

F

Q

D

S

A

P

L

E

J

Place on fold.

Quilt by Judy Sogn
Seattle, Washington

Christmas Tulips

The smartly arranged scarlet tulips in Judy Sogn's quilted wall hanging will brighten your holiday mantel. Inspired by the Rosegay pattern, published in the Spring/Summer 1983 issue of *Quiltmaker*, Judy made a few pattern adjustments and set the design on the diagonal. Suddenly, roses became tulips.

Finished Quilt Size

37½" x 37½"

Fabric Requirements

Dark green	1½ yards*
Dark green print	1¼ yards
Red with white circles	⅜ yard
Red floral print	⅛ yard
Cream with red print	½ yard
Muslin	1 yard
Backing	1¼ yards

*Includes 1 yard for binding.

Number to Cut**

Template A	1 dark green
	4 red floral print
Template B	32 dark green
	16 red with white circles
	4 cream with red print
Template C	8 dark green
Template C rev.	8 dark green
Template D	16 red with white circles
Template E	16 red with white circles
Template F	16 red floral print
Template G	8 cream with red print
Template G rev.	8 cream with red print
Template H	32 muslin
Template I	4 muslin
Template J	32 muslin
Template K	8 muslin
Template L	28 cream with red print
	4 muslin

**See steps 1 and 2 to cut borders and setting triangles before cutting other pieces.

Quilt Top Assembly

1. From dark green print, cut 4 (2½"-wide) inner border strips. Cut 4 (3"-wide) outer border strips.

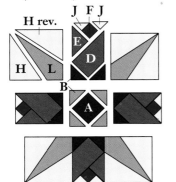

Tulip Block Assembly Diagram

Setting Diagram

Set aside.

2. From muslin, cut 2 (10⅝") squares. Cut each square in half diagonally to make 4 half-square triangles. Set aside.

3. Referring to **Tulip Block Assembly Diagram,** join A, Bs, Ds, Es, Fs, Hs, Js, and Ls into 3 rows. Join rows to complete block.

4. Join Cs to Gs, as shown in **Tulip Strip Diagram.** Join pieced unit to sides of I. Begin stitching from outside edge and stitch up to seam line. Stop and backstitch 1 or 2 stitches. Remove fabric from

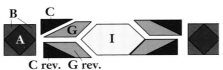

Tulip Strip Diagram

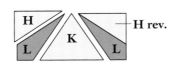

Border Rectangle Assembly Diagram

machine. Align remaining sides and stitch from center to outside edge, backstitching 1 or 2 stitches at the start. Make 2 tulip strips with corner blocks, as shown in **Tulip Strip Diagram,** and 2 without.

Join strips without corner blocks to opposite sides of tulip block. Join strips with corner blocks to top and bottom edges.

5. Join bias edge of muslin triangles cut in Step 2 to sides of quilt.

6. Join 2½"-wide dark green print borders cut in Step 1 to quilt top, mitering corners.

7. Referring to tulip portion of **Tulip Block Assembly Diagram,** make 12 tulips, using Bs, Ds, Es, Fs, and Js.

Join H, K, and L, as shown in **Border Rectangle Assembly Diagram,** to make 8 pieced rectangles.

Alternate 3 tulips with 2 pieced rectangles and join at sides, as shown in **Tulip Border Assembly Diagram.** Join H and L to each end as shown. Repeat to make 4 borders.

Tulip Border Assembly Diagram

8. Join 2 borders to opposite sides of quilt. Begin and end stitching at seam line, backstitching 1 or 2 stitches at beginning and end. Join L to each end of remaining borders, as shown in **Corner Assembly Diagram.** Join borders to quilt in same manner as above. Join borders at corners.

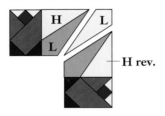

Corner Assembly Diagram

9. Join 3"-wide dark green print borders cut in Step 1 to quilt, mitering corners.

Quilting

Outline-quilt inside seam line of all tulips. Quilt lines from seam junction of H, L, and K, as shown in **Quilting Diagram.** Quilt feather pattern in corners of large triangles of center section. Quilt a ½" cross-hatching pattern for the remainder of open areas of center section. (Judy used an unbroken rope pattern for the dark green print border.)

Finished Edges

Referring to instructions on page 11, make 4½ yards of 2"-wide bias or straight-grain binding from dark green print. Apply binding to quilt edges.

Quilting Diagram

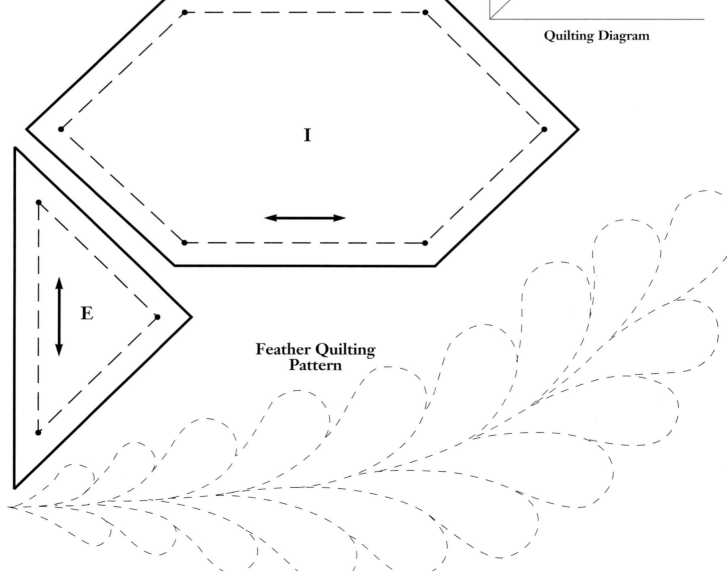

I

E

Feather Quilting Pattern

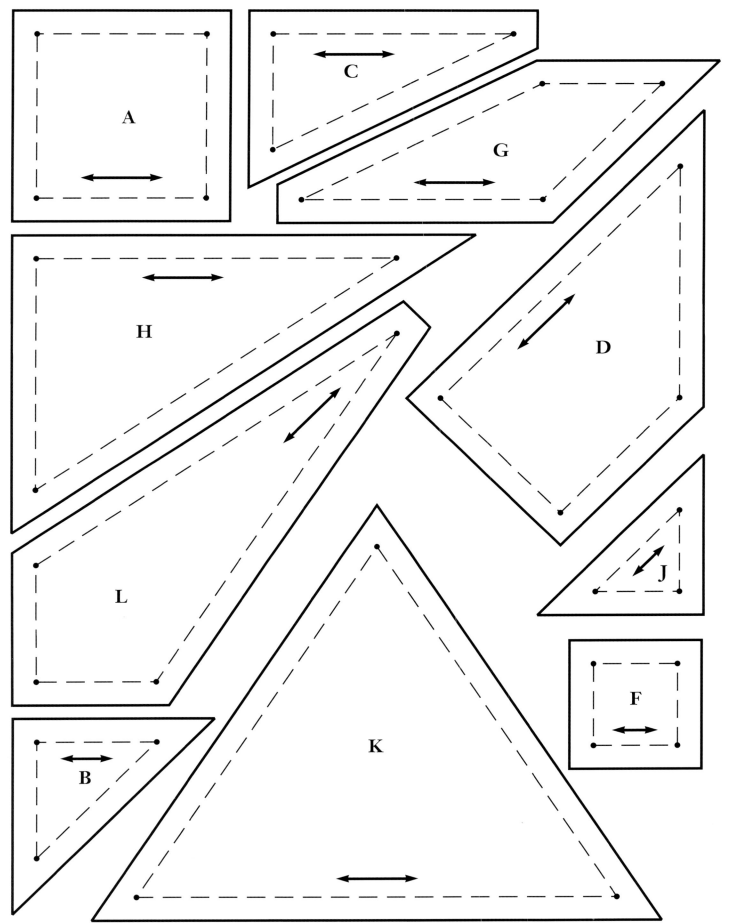

45

Quilt by Linda Nolte Evans
Greenwood Village, Colorado

Bridal Bouquet

Bridal Bouquet was Linda Nolte Evans's first original quilt, made shortly after the birth of her first child. "It expresses the joys and confinements of first motherhood," says Linda. "Many people thought it looked like the top of a wedding cake, which is the reason for the name." Linda stuffed the flower centers to give them dimension and secured them with tiny hand appliqué stitches. She also used a heavy-weight batting to give the quilt a more padded look.

Finished Quilt Size

41½" x 41½"

Fabric Requirements

Muslin	3 yards*
White	⅛ yard
Green	¾ yard
Purple	⅓ yard
Dark yellow	1⅓ yards**
Light yellow	⅓ yard

*Includes fabric for backing.
**Included fabric for binding.

Number to Cut

Template A	16 green
Template A rev.	16 green
Template B	26 green
Template C	15 purple
	7 light yellow
Template D	36 purple
	10 light yellow
	5 white
Template E	10 white
	5 dark yellow
Template F	1 dark yellow
Template G	1 light yellow
Template H	1 light yellow
Template I	1 light yellow
Template J	1 light yellow
Template K	15 dark yellow
	7 purple
Template L	4 dark yellow
Template M	24 dark yellow

Quilt Top Assembly

1. From muslin, cut 1 (34") square. Finger-crease twice to find center.

From green, cut 2 (¾" x 21½") bias strips for center stems and 4 (¾" x 5") bias strips for short side stems. Arrange stems as shown in **Bouquet Placement Diagram** and quilt photograph; appliqué. Appliqué flowers, flower centers, leaves, and bow, as shown. Appliqué bow pieces in the following order: G, F, H, I, J. Stuff flower centers (D) until firm.

2. Arrange tulips (C) with leaves (A) and daisies (E) with leaves (B) in an oval ring around bouquet, as shown in quilt photograph. Oval is approximately 2½" from square's top and bottom edges and 5½" from square's sides. Appliqué pieces.

3. Appliqué tulips and leaves in each corner, as shown in quilt photograph.

4. From muslin, cut 4 (4"-wide) borders and join to sides of quilt and then to top and bottom edges of quilt.

5. Place 6 swags (M) on each border and corner swags (L) in each corner; appliqué. Appliqué 1 D between each swag.

Quilting

Outline-quilt outside seam lines of all appliquéd pieces. An oval of feather quilting surrounds the oval bouquet of flowers on each side, as shown in quilt photograph. Quilt remainder of bouquet area with a 1¼" perpendicular grid. Quilt

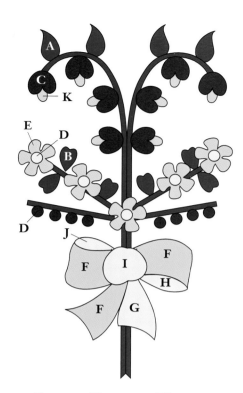

Bouquet Placement Diagram

plumes in each corner and parallel diagonal lines 1¼" apart on the remainder of the quilt.

Finished Edges

Referring to instructions on page 11, make 5 yards of 2"-wide bias or straight-grain binding from dark yellow. Apply binding to quilt edges.

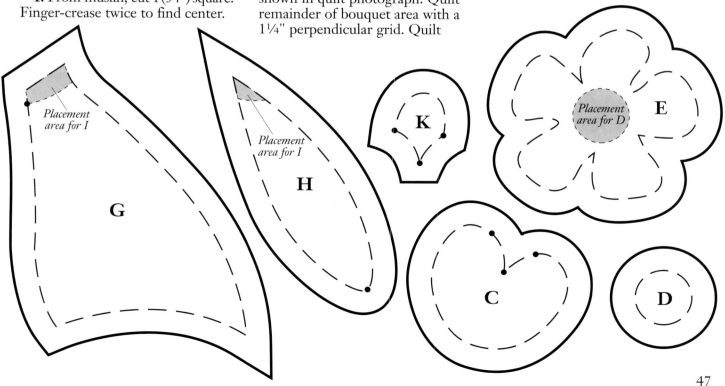

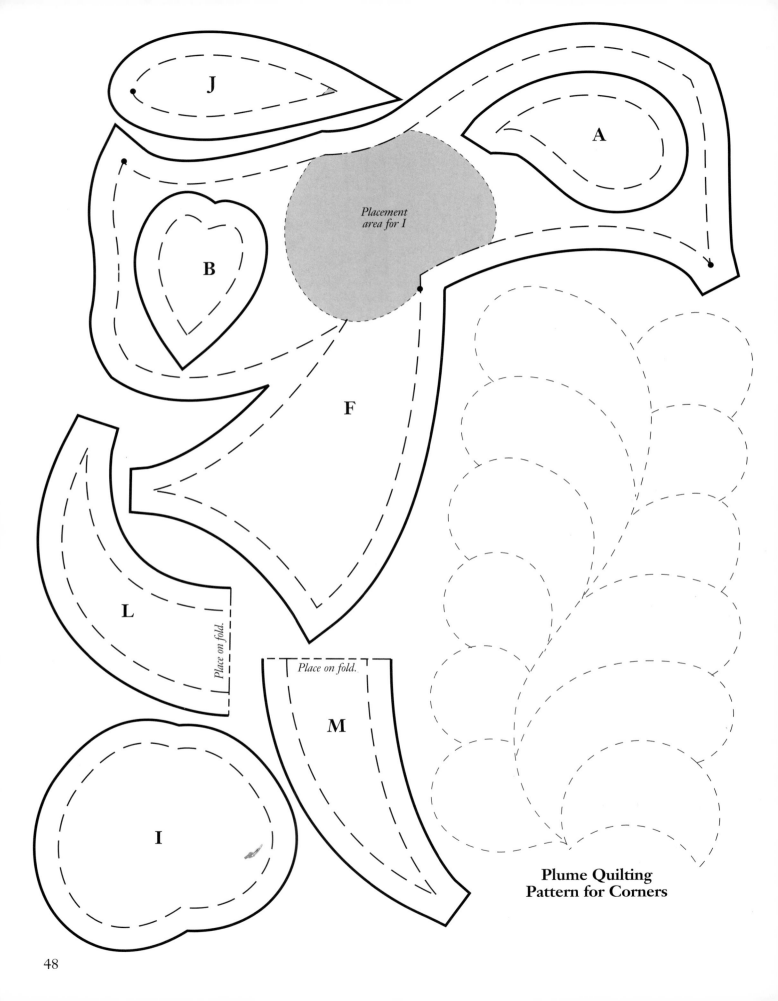

J

A

Placement area for I

B

F

L

Place on fold.

Place on fold.

M

I

Plume Quilting Pattern for Corners

48